W9-AMP-844

Hera

BY VIRGINIA LOH-HAGAN

Gods and goddesses were the main characters of myths. Myths are traditional stories from ancient cultures. Storytellers answered questions about the world by creating exciting explanations. People thought myths were true. Myths explained the unexplainable. They helped people make sense of human behavior and nature. Today, we use science to explain the world. But people still love myths. Myths may not be literally true. But they have meaning. They tell us something about our history and culture.

45th Parallel Press

Published in the United States of America by Cherry Lake Publishing
Ann Arbor, Michigan
www.cherrylakepublishing.com

Content Adviser: Matthew Wellenbach, Catholic Memorial School, West Roxbury, MA
Reading Adviser: Marla Conn MS, Ed., Literacy specialist, Read-Ability, Inc.
Book Designer: Jen Wahi

Photo Credits: © sokolovski/Shutterstock.com, 5; © Pidgorna Ievgeniia/Shutterstock.com, 6; © Howard David Johnson, 2016, 8; © MarcelClemens/Shutterstock.com, 11; © Falcona/Shutterstock.com, 13; © bilwissedition Ltd. & Co. KG/Alamy Stock Photo, 15; © Swapan Photography/Shutterstock.com, 17; © Krivosheev Vitaly/Shutterstock.com, 19; © aaltair/Shutterstock.com, 21; © Boris Diakovsky/Shutterstock.com, 22; © Canon Boy/Shutterstock.com, 25; © Classic Image / Alamy Stock Photo, 27; © Algol/Shutterstock.com, 29; © Howard David Johnson, 2016, Cover; various art elements throughout, shutterstock.com

45th Parallel Press is an imprint of Cherry Lake Publishing.

Library of Congress Cataloging-in-Publication Data

Names: Loh-Hagan, Virginia, author.
Title: Hera / by Virginia Loh-Hagan.
Description: Ann Arbor : Cherry Lake Publishing, [2017] | Series: Gods and
  goddesses of the ancient world | Includes bibliographical references and
  index.
Identifiers: LCCN 2016031182| ISBN 9781634721370 (hardcover) | ISBN
  9781634722698 (pbk.) | ISBN 9781634722032 (pdf) | ISBN 9781634723350
  (ebook)
Subjects: LCSH: Hera (Greek deity)--Juvenile literature. | Goddesses,
  Greek--Juvenile literature. | Mythology, Greek--Juvenile literature.
Classification: LCC BL820.J6 L64 2017 | DDC 292.2/114--dc23
LC record available at https://lccn.loc.gov/2016031182

Printed in the United States of America
Corporate Graphics

ABOUT THE AUTHOR:

Dr. Virginia Loh-Hagan is an author, university professor, former classroom teacher, and curriculum designer. She's a little bit like Hera in that she likes her dogs more than other people's dogs. She lives in San Diego with her very tall husband and very naughty dogs. To learn more about her, visit www.virginialoh.com.

TABLE OF CONTENTS

CHAPTER 1

QUEEN OF GODS

Who is Hera? What did she look like? How did she get married?

Hera was a Greek goddess. She was the goddess of women and marriage. She was the queen of gods. She was married to Zeus. Zeus was the king of the 12 **Olympians**. These gods were the rulers of the gods. They lived on Mount Olympus. Mount Olympus is in Greece. It's the highest mountain in Greece.

Hera's parents were Cronus and Rhea. Her parents were **Titans**. Titans were giant gods. They ruled until the Olympians took over.

Cronus was told that a son would take away his power. So, Cronus ate his children. Rhea saved one child, Zeus. Zeus grew up. He tricked Cronus. He poisoned him. Cronus threw up his children. Zeus brought Hera back to life.

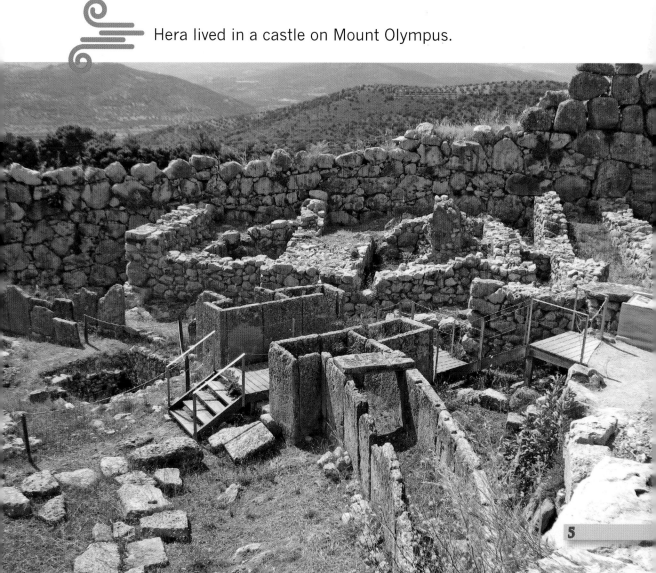

Hera lived in a castle on Mount Olympus.

Hera means "great lady."

Hera wore gold robes and shoes. She had a crown. It was called a **polos**. It was shaped like a tube. It sat high on her head. Hera sat on a golden throne. She had a golden **chariot**. A chariot is a cart with two wheels. It's pulled by animals.

Hera was really beautiful. She was tall. She was classy. She had perfect skin. Zeus fell in love with her. He thought she was the world's most beautiful woman. Hera was his sister. But that didn't matter. Zeus wanted to marry her.

Family Tree

Grandparents: Uranus (Father Sky) and Gaia (Mother Earth)

Parents: Cronus (god of time) and Rhea (goddess of fertility)

Brothers: Zeus (god of the sky), Poseidon (god of the seas), Hades (god of the underworld)

Sisters: Demeter (goddess of the harvest), Hestia (goddess of the hearth and family)

Spouse: Zeus

Children: Ares (god of war), Eileithyia (goddess of childbirth), Enyo (goddess of war), Eris (goddess of strife), Hebe (goddess of youth), Hephaestus (god of fire and craftsmen)

Hera didn't like him at first. She rejected him. Zeus tricked her. He changed into a cuckoo bird. He made a storm. Hera felt sorry for the bird. She took care of the bird. Then, Zeus took his true form. He made her marry him.

Zeus and Hera got married in Samos. Samos is an island in Greece. All of the gods went to the wedding. It was a sacred marriage. They spent 300 years there together. They were happy then.

They went back to Mount Olympus. They weren't happy anymore. They fought a lot. Zeus had many lovers. He loved other goddesses and **mortals**. Mortals are humans. He had many children with different women. This made Hera really jealous.

 Hera was the most beautiful woman on the outside, but she could be mean on the inside.

CHAPTER 2

FEMALE GUARDIAN

What are Hera's powers? How did she protect marriages?

Hera was powerful before she married Zeus. She didn't get power from Zeus. She could move through the air. She couldn't get hurt. She could change her shape. She could change into animals or mortals. She liked changing into birds.

Some people think Hera was a mother goddess. She helped create the world. Hera's milk created the **Milky Way**. The Milky Way is our galaxy. Others say drops of her milk fell to Earth. Her milk created fields of lilies.

Hera blessed and protected marriage. She helped women get married. She made marriages good. She made marriages bad.

The only marriage she couldn't control was her own. That's because Zeus was more powerful.

She represented **monogamy**. That means she was faithful. She never cheated on Zeus.

Hera's power to create the galaxy came from her parents.

All in the Family

Zeus fell in love with Lamia. Zeus and Lamia had children. Hera got jealous. She killed their children. She cursed Lamia. Lamia wasn't able to close her eyes. She had to look at her dead children. Zeus felt sorry for her. He let Lamia take out her eyes and put them back in. This way Lamia could rest her eyes. Seeing her dead children made Lamia go crazy. She got jealous of other mothers. So, she hunted their children. She ate their children. She turned into a monster. She had a snake tail. She had an ugly face.

Controlling childhood is powerful.

She worked with other goddesses to help babies. Demeter helped women get pregnant. Artemis helped women while they were pregnant. Eileithyia helped women have babies. Hera helped mothers care for their children.

CHAPTER 3

MAD LOVE

What upset Hera? How was she as a mother and stepmother? How did she get even?

Hera wasn't always nice. She was easily angered. She was easily offended. She was very **vain**. Vain means she cared a lot about her looks.

A goddess bragged about her hair. She said her hair was prettier than Hera's. Hera got mad. She turned her hair into snakes.

Hera was invited to a wedding. Eris liked to cause trouble. She wasn't invited to the wedding. But she went anyway and brought a golden apple. The apple said, "For the fairest one." Zeus told Paris, the prince of Troy, to decide the fairest goddess. Paris chose Aphrodite. Aphrodite was the goddess of love and beauty. Hera was mad. She fought against Paris in the Trojan War.

Hera was known for being jealous. She was **vengeful**. She harmed others. She wanted to get even. She didn't like that Zeus disrespected marriage. She punished Zeus's lovers.

Hera and Zeus had the longest honeymoon on record.

Real World Connection

Like Hera, jacanas are evil stepmothers. They're waterbirds.
They live in the tropics. Jacana dads make nests. Jacana moms
lay about four eggs. They leave the dads. They look for new dads.
They attack other nests. They don't like having stepchildren.
So, they eat the eggs of other females. Then, they mate with
the dads. They have many lovers. They also have weapons. They
have long legs. They have the longest toes of any birds. They
have long claws. Their big feet let them walk on water. They have
big spurs on each elbow. Spurs are like knives. Jacanas crouch
low. They leap into the air. They hit other females feet first. They
slash with their spurs. They're fighters. They're bigger than
males. They're stronger. They're more aggressive.

Some myths said that Hera gave birth by touching lettuce.

She turned one lover into a bear. She poisoned other lovers. She even killed some.

Hera punished the children of Zeus's lovers. She was an evil stepmother. Zeus's favorite child was Heracles. Heracles's mother was a mortal. Hera sent two snakes to kill Heracles. Heracles was in his crib. He choked the snakes. Hera also tried to drown Heracles in a flood. Zeus punished her. He hung her upside down from the sky. But that didn't stop her. Hera drove Heracles crazy. Heracles killed his wife and children.

Hera wasn't a great mother either. She gave birth to Hephaestus. Hephaestus was ugly. So, Hera rejected him. She threw him off Mount Olympus. Hephaestus landed on an island. The fall damaged his legs. He became **lame**. He didn't walk very well.

Hephaestus wanted to get even with Hera. He made her a magical throne. She sat on it. She couldn't leave. The other gods begged Hephaestus to let her go. He refused. He said, "I have no mother." Finally, Hephaestus let her go. The gods let him marry Aphrodite.

 Hera could cause storms, fights, and deaths.

CHAPTER 4

ALL IN THE EYES

What are Hera's symbols? Why are eyes important to Hera?

Argus was Hera's servant. He had 100 eyes. Hera told him to guard Io. Io was one of Zeus's lovers. She was a mortal. Zeus hid her from Hera. He turned her into a white cow.

Hera begged Zeus to give Io to her. Zeus did. Hera punished Io. She chained her to an olive tree. She made Argus watch over her. This was to stop Zeus from helping her. But Zeus sent Hermes. Hermes was the gods' messenger. Hermes disguised himself as a shepherd. He played music. He told stories. He put Argus's eyes to sleep. Then, he hit him with a stone. Argus died.

This freed Io. Io walked the earth. Hera sent a fly to bother her. The fly stung Io all the time. Io couldn't rest.

Hera rewarded Argus for his work. She took Argus's eyes. She put them in peacock feathers. That's how peacock feathers got their eyes. Peacocks were Hera's special animals. They pulled Hera's chariot. They represented beauty.

Hera is also associated with the cuckoo bird.

The word pomegranate means apple with many seeds.

They were thought to be vain. They represented Hera's pride.

Hera had big, brown eyes. Her symbols are related to eyes. Besides peacocks, her special animals were cows. Cows have big eyes. They represented Hera's watchfulness. Hera watched over everyone. She's sometimes called "cow-eyed." Cows are also motherly. They raise babies with their milk.

Hera's special fruit was pomegranate. Pomegranate juice looks like blood. Blood represents life. Pomegranates are also wedding symbols.

Cross-Cultural Connection

Atahensic is Sky-Woman. She's a Native American sky goddess. She's in charge of marriage, childbirth, and female crafts. She's worshipped by the Iroquois and Huron people. She lived in the sky. She gave birth to twins. The twins were named Hahgwehdiyu and Hahgwehdaetgah. They were good and evil. They fought in her womb. Atahensic died. She fell to the earth. She broke a tree on the way down. She created a hole leading to the earth's center. She was carried down by the wings of birds. The birds carried her to water. A giant turtle kept her body in his shell. Her body made the moon, stars, and sun. Her body also gave corn to the earth. She helped create the earth.

CHAPTER 5

HAIL TO HERA!

What are some stories about Hera? What happens when Hera is dishonored?

There are many myths about Hera.

Hera didn't like vanity in others. Gerana is an example of that. Gerana was queen of the **Pygmy** people. The Pygmies are little people. They worshipped Gerana. Gerana's ego grew. She bragged. She said she was more beautiful than Hera. She didn't honor Hera. That made Hera mad. Hera refused to be disrespected. Hera changed Gerana into the ugliest bird. She changed her into a crane. Gerana was sad. She flew over houses. She looked for her child. Pygmies chased her away. She got into a war with the Pygmies. This war lasted forever.

Hera helped others when it served her needs. Jason's story is an example of that.

Hera had powers to turn mortals into animals when she wanted.

Jason was the son of a king. But his uncle stole the throne. His uncle was named Pelias. Pelias jailed Jason's father.

Explained By Science

Some people are extremely jealous. They have a medical disorder. They have the Othello syndrome. Othello is a character from a play by William Shakespeare. Othello was really jealous. He killed his wife. He killed himself. People with Othello syndrome believe their partner is cheating on them. They don't have real proof. They search for evidence. They question their partner. They test their partner's love. Debbi Wood might have Othello syndrome. Wood checks her partner's phone and e-mails. She makes him take a lie detector test. She doesn't let him look at other women. She's been called the world's most jealous woman.

Hera, and many of the gods, could get very jealous.

He wanted to kill Jason. But Jason's mom saved him.
He grew up. He wanted to take back the throne.

Hera didn't like Pelias. Pelias didn't honor Hera.
Pelias killed his stepmother. He did it at Hera's temple.
This stopped people from worshipping at her temple.
Hera was mad. She vowed to get even with Pelias.

Hera needed a hero. She tested Jason. She turned into an old woman. She waited by a river. She asked Jason to carry her across. Jason did. Hera revealed herself. She agreed to help Jason.

Pelias told Jason to get the Golden **Fleece**. A fleece is a woolen coat. A monster protected the Fleece. Hera helped Jason get an army and ship. She let Jason use wood from Zeus's magical forests. The wood could speak. It helped Jason find his way. Hera made Medea love Jason. Medea was a witch. She gave him a special potion to fight monsters. Jason got the Fleece with Hera's help. Jason gave the Fleece to Pelias. Then Jason killed Pelias. Hera got her revenge.

Don't anger the goddesses. Hera had great powers. And she knew how to use them.

 The Argonauts were named after their ship, the Argo.

DID YOU KNOW?

- Ancient Romans worshipped gods. Juno was the Roman version of Hera. The month of June is named after Juno.

- Ancient Greeks dedicated a temple to Hera. The temple was at Samos. This may have been the first temple dedicated to a goddess.

- Zeus got Echo to distract Hera. Echo led Hera away. Echo flattered her. Hera found out she was being tricked. She cursed Echo. Echo could only repeat the words of others.

- Hera had other names. She's been called "Goat-Eater," "Cow-Eyed," and "White-Armed."

- Hera's name is connected to the word hora. Hora means "season." It's interpreted as meaning ready for marriage.

- Sporting contests were held to honor Hera. They were called Heraean Games. Only women and girls could compete. Champions won olive crowns. They won cow meat from the animal sacrificed to Hera.

- Yearly marriage festivals were held to honor Hera. Couples pretended to be Zeus and Hera. They acted out their wedding.

CONSIDER THIS!

TAKE A POSITION Hera did a lot of mean things because she was jealous. What made her jealous? Do you think her actions were justifiable? Did her punishments fit the crime? Argue your point with reasons and evidence.

SAY WHAT? Explain how Hera's powers were both good and evil. How did she use her powers in good ways? How did she use her powers in evil ways?

THINK ABOUT IT! Hera was the goddess of marriage. How was Hera a good wife? How was she a bad wife? Do you think she was a good goddess of marriage?

LEARN MORE

O'Connor, George. *Athena: Grey-Eyed Goddess*. New York; First Second, 2011.

Temple, Teri, and Robert Squier (illustrator). *Hera: Queen of the Gods, Goddess of Marriage*. North Mankato, MN: Child's World, 2013.

GLOSSARY

chariot (CHAR-ee-uht) two-wheeled cart pulled by animals

fleece (FLEES) woolen coat

lame (LAYM) injured

Milky Way (MIL-kee WAY) the galaxy with our solar system

monogamy (muh-NAHG-uh-mee) being faithful to one person

mortals (MOR-tuhlz) humans

Olympians (uh-LIM-pee-uhnz) rulers of the gods who lived on Mount Olympus

polos (POH-lohz) high, tubelike crowns worn by great goddesses

Pygmy (PIG-mee) race of little people

Titans (TYE-tunz) giant gods who ruled before Olympians took over

vain (VAYN) caring a lot about one's looks

vengeful (VENJ-ful) seeking revenge in mean ways

INDEX